How to Be a

Pirate

Written by
John Malam

NATIONAL GEOGRAPHIC
Washington, D.C.

Illustrated by
Dave Antram

© The Salariya Book Company Ltd MMIV
Please visit the Salariya Book Company at:
www.salariya.com

First published in North America in 2005 by
NATIONAL GEOGRAPHIC SOCIETY
1145 17th Street, N.W.
Washington, D.C. 20036-4688

Trade ISBN: 0-7922-7448-2
Library ISBN: 0-7922-7497-0

Library of Congress Cataloging-in-Publication Data available on request.

Printed in China

Series created and designed by David Salariya
Penny Clarke, Consultant Editor
Karen Barker Smith, Editor

For the National Geographic Society
Bea Jackson, Art Director
Virginia Ann Koeth, Project Editor

Stuart Slade, Fact Consultant
Education Officer at the National Maritime Museum in London, England

Photographic credits
t=top b=bottom c=center l=left r=right

The Art Archive / Château-Musée de Dieppe / Dagli
Orti: 15
The Art Archive / Museum für Völkerkunde Vienna /
Dagli Orti: 211
© National Maritime Museum, London: 18, 19, 21r, 28

Every effort has been made to trace copyright holders.
The Salariya Book Company apologizes for any uninten-
tional omissions and would be pleased, in such cases, to
add an acknowledgment in future editions.

One of the world's largest nonprofit scientific and educational organizations, the National Geographic Society was founded in 1888
"for the increase and diffusion of geographic knowledge." Fulfilling this mission, the Society educates and inspires millions every day
through its magazines, books, television programs, videos, maps and atlases, research grants, the National Geographic Bee, teacher
workshops, and innovative classroom materials. The Society is supported through membership dues, charitable gifts, and income from
the sale of its educational products. This support is vital to National Geographic's mission to increase global understanding and promote
conservation of our planet through exploration, research, and education.

For more information, please call 1-800-NGS LINE (647-5463) or write to the following address:
National Geographic Society
1145 17th Street N.W.
Washington, D.C. 20036-4688 U.S.A.
Visit the Society's Web site at www.nationalgeographic.com.

Pirates Needed

Do you want to go to faraway, interesting places, meet new people, eat their food, learn their language…and get rich?

Adventurers are needed for a trip to the Spanish Main, on board the sloop *Dolphin*, which sails out of Port Royal on the sunny island of Jamaica. You must be healthy, quick with a cutlass, good at rope-work, and possess a keen eye for spotting valuables. A fine singing voice would be an asset.

Your main duties will include:

- keeping the *Dolphin* all shipshape—not a thing out of place and everything in good condition

- using axes, swords, pikes, pistols, and grenades

- above all, obeying the rules of the ship

If you think you can do the job, attend the meeting at the Singing Sailors Inn, where the crew of the *Dolphin* will be chosen.

Contents

What Applicants Should Know	5
Skills a Pirate Needs	6
Life on Board	8
Captain and Crew	10
Clothing	12
Navigating	14
Pirate Flags	16
Pirate Attack!	18
Booty for All	20
Food and Drink	22
A Safe Haven	24
Passing the time	26
Punishment	28
Your Interview	30
Glossary	31
Index	32
Further Reading	32
Have You Got the Job?	32

What Applicants Should Know

So you think you have what it takes to be a pirate? Be prepared for a dangerous journey—the islands of the Caribbean Sea might have sun, sand, and shimmering silver, but you're not going there for a vacation. It is around the year 1700, and you'll be going to a part of the New World where every last scoundrel, thief, and drunk has fled. Port Royal, on the south coast of Jamaica, is where the *Dolphin* sails from. Port Royal is a safe haven for pirates and all who live outside the law. It has become the major city in the region with a population of about 3,000. Port Royal is sheltered from storms. On fair days ships leave her deep harbor for the Spanish Main. This is the name given to the area that stretches from the north coast of South America to Florida in North America.

The Caribbean Sea, 1680

Skills a Pirate Needs

Living on a ship doesn't suit everyone. Think hard before you decide to board the *Dolphin*. Once she's at sea there's no turning back until her hold is filled with treasure. It's tough work keeping the ship in good condition, day and night. Be prepared to go without sleep until your work is done. When a ship is attacked and taken, you'll need your sea legs and great courage to protect yourself and win the fight.

Tying knots

Knots are important on board—they ▶ can join two pieces of rope together, make loops, or tie things to parts of the ship.

A bowline makes the best loop. It won't slip.

A head for heights?

▲ You'll need to be brave and have a firm grip to climb the rigging in all kinds of weather and to act as the lookout.

Shipboard Jobs

▲ Life is often very busy on board ship—one minute you could be sewing sailcloth, the next you might be busy with rope-work, tying a bowline knot at the end of a mooring rope or using bend knots to join ropes together.

Bowline knot for
making loops

Start   Finish

Only if you
get it right!

Bend knots
for joining
ropes

Carrick bend knot   Sheet bend knot

Rowing and sword-fighting

▼ You'll need strong arms and a strong back to row the sloop's boat toward another ship. The harder you row, the sooner you will reach your prize.

▼ Once aboard the prize ship you must fight with your cutlass. This is a heavy sword with a sharp blade and a basket-shaped guard to protect your hand and wrist. Use it for slashing and hacking at the enemy.

Life on Board

You might be at sea for weeks before you sight a prize ship. Until then, your life will consist of routine, boring jobs. Singing chanteys (songs sung by sailors) will help pass the time. You'll lift the crew's spirits if you can whistle a tune on a pipe. Everyone has a job to do: repairing the deck, pouring molten lead to make musket balls, or preparing fresh fish to eat. The gold and riches you seek are never forgotten though.

Foresails Mainsail

Pirate sloop

◀ Many Caribbean pirates sail in fast ships called sloops. They have a single mast with a large mainsail and smaller foresails.

Sing along, men... We're off to seek our fortune, lads...

Only one more day together...

A cat hunting rats on board ship

Treasure ship

◄ Keep a close watch for a prize— a slow-sailing galleon bound for Spain. Its cargo will be treasure from places like Peru and Mexico.

Then no more gales or heavy weather!

Keeping water out

▼ The ship is leaking! Don't panic. All wooden ships let in water through small gaps in their hulls. It collects in the ship's bilges. Pumps suck it up and pour it into buckets. Bilgewater stinks of rot and filth, so don't spill it on deck as you empty the buckets over the side.

Bilge pump

▼ One never-ending job is caulking timbers. This means pushing shredded rope, called oakum, into gaps in the hull. It is then glued in place with black pitch, which sets hard to make a water-tight seal.

Ramming iron

Caulking mallet

Unwelcome guests

◄ On some ships there are more rats than seamen. They gnaw their way through ropes and timbers, eat the crew's food, and spread disease. The ship's cats kill many, but if you see a rat, toss it to the sharks.

Captain and Crew

The captain expects every seaman to know his place and do his duty the best he can. In return for hard work and loyalty you will get a share of any treasure taken. The size of your share depends on the job you do. There will be no arguments about it, since you must keep to the rules–ship's articles–you signed when you joined the ship.

Choosing the captain

▼ Before a ship sails, the crew votes on which one of them should be captain. Scuffles may break out, but one man is finally chosen. He promises riches for all.

Vote me cap'n, lads, an' I'll make ye all rich!

Your captain

▼ He is the ship's commander. He gives orders during battle and expects seamen to do as he says. He's been voted captain because the crew looks up to him as a strong leader.

Cutlass

Carpenter   Surgeon   Seaman   Cabin boy   Musician

Mutiny!

If at any time the captain shows signs of weakness, such as refusing to attack a prize ship, or is cruel to his men, the crew may mutiny and choose another man as captain.

You can have my vote!

I'd rather have a rat as my cap'n!

The quartermaster

▶ The quartermaster is second in command and will take charge of the rations and captured booty. He is the only man allowed to flog (whip) a seaman. This is usually done with a cat-o'-nine-tails— a whip with nine knotted lashes.

Cat-o'-nine-tails

The ship's articles

▼ Every seaman must sign the ship's articles (*below*) and swear on the holy Bible to obey the rules. Brawling, cheating at cards, and cowardice are forbidden. The rules also state how the treasure is to be shared.

Cook   Boatswain

Master gunner   Seamen

Clothing

You are likely to own only one set of clothes. You'll work, fight, and sleep in them. New clothes are expensive, and the only way you'll get clothes like a rich man is by stealing some from a wealthy seafarer. Like the other seamen on board, you will have clothes made of heavy wool or perhaps stitched together from scraps of canvas sailcloth. You will also be barefoot. You will wear loose-fitting trousers, cut off below the knee, and a thigh-length shirt or coat.

Sailcloth for clothes

▼ Sailcloth is a thick, rough canvas woven from hemp fibers. Old pieces of sailcloth can be used to make long-lasting clothes.

This sail has more holes than my shirt.

◄ Before you board a prize ship, give your clothes an extra-thick coating of black tar. Your enemy's sword will slip off the tar. This may save your skin.

Keeping clean

Freshwater is for drinking, not for washing clothes or bodies. If you want to wash yourself, use rainwater collected in tubs. If the ship drops anchor, take a dip in the sea—but beware of sharks.

This bilgewater is filthy!

Fashion

Although pirates wear hoops in their ears, made of brass or even gold, they sell most of the jewelry they capture from their enemies.

Rags and riches

Cocked hat with a feather

Leather strap for holding weapons

Velvet jacket

Silk sash

Trousers tied at the knee

Stockings

Buckled shoes

▲ The captain has fine clothes, taken from his victims.

▶ Your clothes are canvas rags, smeared in black tar to protect you from the cold and wet. You will wear them until they rot away. If you lose a leg in a fight, a carpenter will carve a wooden peg that you can strap to your stump.

13

Navigating

The navigator uses the best scientific tools available to find the ship's position at sea. In the daytime he measures the height of the sun in relation to the horizon. At night, the moon and stars help him to fix the ship's course. By knowing where the ship is, the direction of her course he can work out and plot it on charts. The captain decides where the ship sails.

The anchor

To stop the ship, her iron anchor is ▶ dragged along the seabed until it catches on a rock or sturdy object. In heavy weather, a firm anchor can stop the ship running aground.

Our course is straight and true.

Land ho!

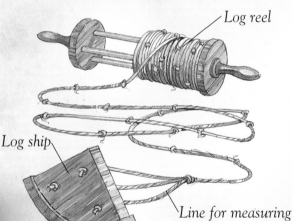

Log reel

Log ship

Line for measuring the ship's speed

▲ Speed at sea is measured in knots. A knotted line (*above*) is unwound over the side. By measuring the number of knots that unwind in thirty seconds, the speed of the ship can be measured.

▲ The captain uses his dividers to measure the distance sailed from day to day (*above*), making sure that all is well with the course.

Anchor

The compass never lies.

Navigation tools

▼ In fog you must watch for rocks and other dangers. A sailor will lower a lead weight to the seabed to measure the water depth in fathoms. A fathom is the length between his outstretched arms—6 feet (1.83 m).

▼ Other instruments include the compass for finding direction and the captain's telescope, which allows him to see land and ships from a great distance. The dividers measure distance on the charts, and the backstaff is used by the navigator to work out the ship's position. Often, navigational tools are stolen from captured ships.

A 17th-century compass

Pirate Flags

Be proud of the Jolly Roger, the flag the *Dolphin* flies as she engages an enemy ship. The flag's skull and crossbones are symbols understood by seamen of all nations. They stand for death and violence. Many a prize ship surrenders without a fight as soon as it spies the Jolly Roger at the top of the main mast.

A flag to fear

▼ If you're asked to make a Jolly Roger, the captain will tell you what design he wants. The bolder the design, the more it will frighten your enemy.

Skull and crossbones design

Raising the Jolly Roger

▼ In most battles, surprise is the best tactic – your ship wouldn't stand a chance in open battle. Wait until the last moment to raise your flag. Your enemy will not know whether you are friend or foe until it is too late.

Now you know who we are!

You will see vessels called "privateers," ▶ which fly the flags of their countries. They are private warships. Their governments give them permission to plunder enemy ships, so in a way they are really just pirates like you.

Your prize is in sight

When your enemy sees the Jolly Roger flying from the main mast, she may try to escape. But your sloop, the *Dolphin*, is small and fast and you will soon be alongside her.

Different Jolly Rogers

◀ The skull and crossbones. A red background means all your enemies will die.

◀ The flag of John Rackham, known as "Calico Jack" because he wore striped pants.

◀ The flag of Edward Teach, known as "Blackbeard."

◀ The flag of Henry Every, known as "Long Ben." He raided ships in the Red Sea and Indian Ocean.

◀ The two flags of Bartholomew Roberts. The letters on the top flag are the initials of men against whom he has vowed revenge. On the bottom flag a skeleton hands an hourglass to his prey, to show that time is running out.

Flags of three nations

Britain

France

Spain

Pirate Attack!

Now the prize ship has seen your Jolly Roger and knows the *Dolphin* is a pirate ship. The next few minutes will be dangerous, as you board the ship and come face to face with your victims. Some of them may turn against their own officers and change sides, hoping for a share of the ship's riches. The seamen who resist you will meet a bloody end, killed by a sword, ax, or gun. Pirates are not known for their mercy.

Guns at sea

▼ When you're in action you must keep your gunpowder dry. You will use a flintlock musket when shooting from a distance and a flintlock pistol for close combat. Both weapons shoot heavy balls of lead, but the pistol can also be used for clubbing your enemies.

Grenades

◀ Light the fuse, throw it, take cover, and wait for the grenade to explode, flinging lead shot in every direction.

Avast, ye Spaniards!

Have mercy upon us!

A flintlock pistol

Metal butt for clubbing

Chain-shot

Cannonballs joined by chain

◀ Chain-shot is fired into an enemy's rigging. With torn sails, a ship is dead in the water.

> No booty, no reward!

Firing a cannon

▼ Sloops like the *Dolphin* carry small cannons that are used just to frighten the enemy—the last thing you want to do is sink the prize before you have plundered it! It takes three men to operate a cannon, firing one iron cannonball every ten minutes over a distance of about 492 feet (150 m).

▼ In hand-to-hand fighting use axes, swords, daggers and pikes (like spears). Keep their blades and points sharp to cut through your enemy's tough leather clothes.

Cutlass with steel blade

Basket hilt to protect your hand

Booty for All

With an enemy ship under your control, it's time to find out what treasure she carries. The ship may contain chests of gold, silver coins, jewelry, or other cargo you can steal. The quartermaster will take charge of whatever booty is found. He will share it among the seamen, according to the ship's articles, at the end of the voyage and not before.

Stealing provisions

▼ Take gunpowder to add to your supplies, axes and swords that are sharper, and guns that fire better. Freshwater, food, alcohol, and tobacco are always welcome.

▲ Pirates look after each other. If you lose a limb, or are otherwise injured, you'll be given an extra share of the booty to make up for your suffering.

Precious metal

The Spanish took gold objects from ▶ the peoples of the New World. They melted them down to make coins, which were sent back to Europe on ships.

Medicine

◀ A medicine chest with potions, ointments, oils, and doctor's tools could save your life—take it too!

The ultimate prize

▼ The greatest prize of all may well be the enemy ship herself. Any members of her crew who do not agree to join you will be cast adrift in a longboat. The quartermaster will take command, and the ship will sell for a good price.

You'll find no more valuables on my ship.

Stop your lies, captain!

▼ If your prize is a galleon from the Spanish treasure fleet, her hold may be full of coins. Look for gold doubloons and silver pesos. A peso is worth eight *reales* (royals), so pirates call them pieces of eight.

A silver piece of eight

Gold lip-plug from Peru

Food and Drink

The *Dolphin* carries a good supply of food and drink, hopefully. Enough food at least until you take on new supplies at port or seize a ship and raid its stores. Fresh food doesn't last long at sea. Even dried food turns bad in the damp air of the ship's hold. Only heavily salted fish and meat will last the length of the trip and you'll soon get tired of that. Cook will do his best to hide the bad taste with spices and will make strongly flavored drinks to wash your meals down.

Bottled beer

◀ Freshwater turns foul on a long voyage, so the ship carries bottles of ale for the crew to drink with their food.

What foul poison do you call this, cook?

A turtle is killed with a wooden club

▲ Live sea turtles are kept in the hold until needed for food. Their meat is often grilled over a smoky fire.

Scurvy

If you're at sea for a long time you will not eat many vegetables or much fresh fruit. This means you run the risk of scurvy—a disease caused by a lack of vitamin C. Watch out for these symptoms: blotches and sores on the skin, pimples on the gums, teeth falling out, and feeling weak.

Rum ration

▶ You'll get a daily swig of rumbullion, a sweet alcohol made from molasses. The English call it "rum."

A pirate's menu

▼ The *Dolphin* sails with caged hens, which provide fresh meat and eggs. Fresh fish can be caught from the sea too, but on days when there is no fresh food, you must chew on ship's biscuits. These are known as "hardtack" because they're so tough. Don't complain if you find a maggot in them (they eat the biscuits, too).

It's sea turtle. Eat it and be grateful!

Caged hens

Hardtack

▶ Salamagundi is a stew made from roast meat (turtle, duck, hen, or pigeon) chopped into chunks and soaked in wine. Vegetables (cabbage and onions) and occasionally fruit (mangoes) are thrown in, along with vinegar, salt, garlic, pepper, and mustard. It's spicy!

Salamagundi spiced stew

A Safe Haven

Like many other pirate ships of the Spanish Main, the *Dolphin* regards the lawless Jamaican town of Port Royal as her home port. The town has many wealthy merchants who will buy your looted gold, silver, and jewelry cheaply. They will sell it in London for a high price and with their profits buy supplies of food and other goods to sell to pirates in Port Royal.

Smoking allowed

You can't smoke while you're on board ▶ ship for fear of setting it on fire—you have to make do with chewing tobacco instead. But when in port you can light up a clay pipe and smoke if you like.

These men have more money than sense.

Life's luxuries

▲ You can afford to enjoy life now. Ask for a bottle of fine wine, but check that the cork is well tied on or else the contents could be sour.

▲ You'll be welcome in the port's taverns, where you'll find entertainment to suit every seaman. But be warned. These places are filled with thieves and tricksters—both men and women—who will want your money.

Clay tobacco pipe

What to do with your money

▼ Cheats will try to swindle you out of your money at cards. They use weighted dice and a marked deck. Unless you catch them at it, you'll never know you've been tricked.

Back in port at last!

Sworn to secrecy

▼ You've heard stories that pirates sometimes bury their booty, but you tend to spend all of your captured wealth.

Passing the Time

There's a lot of hard work to do on board the *Dolphin*—but you will have some time to relax and enjoy yourself. You could practice your skills as an artist, a singer, a dancer, or a musician. Or you could let a fellow seaman give you a tattoo. You might even catch up on some much needed sleep. While the captain sleeps in his private cabin, you'll sleep on the deck or in the hold among the ship's equipment. Your bed will be a hammock or a straw mattress.

Now hop on your left foot.

Easier said than done, mate!

Keeping busy at sea

▶ Some of the men scratch pictures on to animal bones or teeth. Black soot rubbed over the marks makes them stand out.

Whale tooth

Dancing the night away

▲ Anyone for a dance? At the end of the day, when work is done, musicians strike up a lively tune on the fiddle and the squeeze-box. They will play a dance tune with steps that are easy to learn.

Settling an argument

◀ Be prepared to settle an argument with your bare knuckles. While you fight, the rest of the ship's crew will be betting on who they think will win, even though the Ship's Articles forbid gambling.

Silly old fool!

Exotic creatures

▼ Macaws can be taught to speak.

The exotic animals of the New World make excellent companions on board ship.

▼ Monkeys can learn tricks.

Tattoo

Tattooing

▶ Some seamen decorate their skin with pictures by pricking it with needles. Then they rub pigments (colors) into the designs. As the skin heals, a colored picture is left under the skin.

Punishment

As long as you are on board the *Dolphin* you follow the ship's articles. If you break the rules you will be punished, which is usually by flogging. The quartermaster will whip your back with a cat-o'-nine-tails. This will cut your back to ribbons. Another punishment is keelhauling, where the unfortunate seaman is dragged underwater from one side of the ship to the other. If he doesn't drown, the man may well die from the cuts he got as his body was pulled over the razor-sharp barnacles that grow on the ship's hull.

▼ The cat-o'-nine-tails is made by the man to be flogged, as part of his punishment.

Hanging
◀ Pray that you are never caught and "turned off the cart." This means death by hanging.

Thirty-four...

Nine lengths of knotted rope

Torture

▶ If you are a pirate caught by the law you may be tortured. Will you take the pain, or will you tell them where your booty is?

Hung from a gibbet

Gibbet

▶ The body of an executed pirate swings from a gibbet. The body is clamped inside a metal cage so it will still look human as it rots. Sometimes it is coated in tar to make it rot even more slowly. The grisly remains are placed at the water's edge to warn others who may be tempted into a life of piracy.

A marooned sailor watches his ship sail away

Marooned

▶ Pirates sometimes punish traitors or rivals by leaving them on a remote island. When the supplies the crew gave you run out, you will have to find for food or starve.

Your Interview

Answer these questions to test your knowledge, then look at page 32 to find out if you have what it takes to get the job.

Q1 What are musket balls made of?
A gold
B silver
C lead

Q2 What is a bowline?
A a knot
B a weapon
C a dance

Q3 How do you find your buried booty?
A with a lantern
B with a map
C with a cutlass

Q4 What type of songs will you sing?
A chanteys
B jigs
C reels

Q5 What is salmagundi?
A spiced beer
B spiced stew
C a type of torture

Q6 What do you do with "hardtack?"
A fire it from your pistol
B stamp on it before it bites
C eat it

Q7 What is keelhauling?
A being dragged around the deck
B being dragged under the ship
C being dragged to the top of the mast

Q8 Who is second in command?
A the quartermaster
B the musician
C you

Glossary

Backstaff. A tool for working out the position of a ship.

Bilges. The lowest compartment of a ship.

Booty. Stolen goods.

Calico. A plain white cotton fabric.

Cat-o'-nine-tails. A whip used for punishment.

Cutlass. A sword with a basket-shaped guard to protect hand and wrist.

Doubloon. Spanish gold coin.

Galleon. A large merchant ship.

Hold. The area used for supplies and sleeping quarters under the deck.

Knot. A unit of measurement for a ship's speed.

Lip-plug. An ornament worn in a hole cut through the lower lip.

Marooned. To be abandoned.

Mutiny. When the crew overrules the captain and takes control of the ship.

New World. North and South America in relation to Europe.

Oakum. Shredded rope used for sealing gaps in the ship's hull.

Piece of eight. The nickname for a silver coin worth eight *reales*.

Pitch. A black, resinlike liquid.

Privateer. A type of pirate ship whose crew works for a government.

Prize ship. A ship taken as wages or a reward.

Sailcloth. Tough canvas for sails. Also used for making long-lasting clothes.

Sea legs. A term used to indicate the ability to keep balanced and move around well on a ship.

Shot. Small, lead pellets used in shotguns.

Sloop. A small, fast sailing ship.

Tar. Boiled-down pitch. Also a slang name for a sailor.

Tattoo. A picture drawn by inserting pigments (colors) under the skin.

Index

B
"Blackbeard" (Edward Teach),
   pirate flag of, 17
booty. *See* treasure (booty)

C
"Calico Jack" (John Rackham),
   pirate flag of, 17
captain, 10–11, 13–16, 26
clothing, 12–13, 19, 31
cutlass,   3, 7, 10, 19, 31

E
entertainment, 8, 24–27
Every, Henry ("Long Ben"),
   pirate flag of, 17

F
flags, 16–18
   of specific pirates, 17
food, 8–9, 20, 22–24, 29

J
jobs aboard ship, 3, 6–11, 14–15,
Jolly Roger, 16–18

L
"Long Ben" (Henry Every),
   pirate flag of, 17

N
navigation, 14–15

O
oakum, 9, 31

P
piece of eight, 21, 31
privateers, 16, 31
prize ship, 7–9, 11–12, 16–21, 31
punishment, 11, 28–29, 31

Q
quartermaster, 11, 20–21, 28

R
Rackham, John ("Calico
   Jack"), pirate flag of, 17
Roberts, Bartholomew,
   pirate flags of, 17
rope, 3, 6–7, 9, 28

S
ship's articles, 10–11, 20, 28
Spanish Main, 3, 5, 24

T
Teach, Edward ("Blackbeard"),
   pirate flag of, 17
treasure (booty), 6, 8–11, 19–21,
   24–25, 29, 31

W
weapons, 3, 7–8, 10–13, 18–20, 31

Further Reading

Maynard, Christopher and Griffey, Harriet. *Pirates: Raiders of the High Seas (DK Readers)*. Dorling Kindersley Publishing, 1998.
Platt, Richard and Chambers, Tina. *Pirates (Eyewitness)*. Dorling Kindersley Publishing, 2004.

Have You Got the Job?

Count up your correct answers (*below right*) and find out if you got the job.

Your score:

8 Congratulations: a pirate's life is obviously the one for you.
7 Not quite ready: but if someone drops out before the *Dolphin* leaves port, you can join us.
5-6 Promising: you have the right qualities—try again when we're back in port.

3-4 Not ready yet: your sea legs are too shaky.
Fewer than 3 Too bad: you'd better stay on sold ground.

1 (C) page 8, 18
2 (A) page 6–7
3 (B) page 25
4 (A) page 8
5 (B) page 23
6 (C) page 23
7 (B) page 28
8 (A) page 11